Crossword Bible Studies
Romans

King James Version

Crossword Bible Studies - Romans: King James Version
Copyright © 2012 Christy Bower
www.ChristyBower.com
ISBN-13: 978-1479147366
ISBN-10: 1479147362

Cover image © iStockphoto.com / Tatyana Ogryzko
The 1611 edition of the King James Version (KJV) is in the public domain.

All clues are taken directly from the 1611 edition of the King James Version (KJV).
Crossword Bible Studies - Romans (KJV) © 2012 Christy Bower
These puzzles are reproducible if you purchased the book.
www.CrosswordBibleStudies.com

Thank You

Thank you for purchasing this volume of *Crossword Bible Studies*. You just put a meal on my table. And your support enables me to continue to produce other resources to help people grow in their faith.

Reproducible Puzzles

If you purchased this book, the author grants you the right to reproduce the puzzles for your family, church, or school. Please do not remove or alter the copyright information, instructions, and web address at the bottom of each page. You may not distribute digital copies and you may not resell either printed or digital copies.

Studying the Bible Can Be Fun

You'll have so much fun working these crossword puzzles; you'll never know it's a Bible study. Each puzzle is based on one chapter of the Bible and the clues are taken directly from the 1611 edition of the King James Version (KJV). The verse reference is provided with each puzzle clue, so all you have to do is look up the answer in your Bible.

Don't have a KJV? Check out www.ChristyBower.com to view, print, or download the text for each chapter or an entire book of the Bible.

Note: The clues are taken from the 1611 edition of the King James Version because it is in the public domain and free of copyright restrictions. Newer versions of the KJV have been edited over the years and may reflect slightly different wording in places. Be aware of this if you are looking up clues in a newer edition.

All clues are taken directly from the 1611 edition of the King James Version (KJV).
Crossword Bible Studies - Romans (KJV) © 2012 Christy Bower
These puzzles are reproducible if you purchased the book.
www.CrosswordBibleStudies.com

Romans 1 (KJV)

Across

2. they glorified him not as God, neither were _____ (1:21)
4. without ceasing I make _____ of you always in my prayers (1:9)
5. I am ready to preach the _____ to you that are at Rome (1:15)
6. for _____ to the faith among all nations (1:5)
11. and _____ and served the creature more than the Creator (1:25)
12. they which commit such things are worthy of _____ (1:32)
13. through the lusts of their own _____ (1:24)
14. therein is the _____ of God revealed from faith to faith (1:17)
17. wickedness, _____, maliciousness (1:29)
19. I am not _____ of the gospel of Christ (1:16)
20. changed the glory of the uncorruptible God into an _____ made like to corruptible man (1:23)
22. if by any means now at length I might have a _____ journey (1:10)
23. that your _____ is spoken of throughout the whole world (1:8)
24. For the _____ things of him from the creation of the world are clearly seen (1:20)
25. I would not have you _____, brethren (1:13)

Down

1. that I may be _____ together with you by the mutual faith (1:12)
3. For the wrath of God is revealed from heaven against all _____ (1:18)
4. that which may be known of God is _____ in them (1:19)
7. _____ of evil things (1:30)
8. Without understanding, _____, without natural affection (1:31)
9. _____ themselves to be wise, they became fools (1:22)
10. God gave them over to a _____ mind (1:28)
15. To all that be in _____, beloved of God (1:7)
16. by the _____ from the dead (1:4)
18. that I may impart unto you some _____ gift (1:11)
21. Paul, a servant of Jesus Christ, called to be an _____ (1:1)

Romans 1 (KJV)

All clues are taken directly from the 1611 edition of the King James Version (KJV).
Crossword Bible Studies - Romans (KJV) © 2012 Christy Bower
These puzzles are reproducible if you purchased the book.
www.CrosswordBibleStudies.com

Romans 2 (KJV)

Across

2. Therefore thou art _____ (2:1)
4. An instructor of the _____, a teacher of babes (2:20)
5. Tribulation and _____, upon every soul of man that doeth evil (2:9)
6. But unto them that are contentious, and do not obey the _____ (2:8)
8. For not the _____ of the law are just before God, but the doers of the law (2:13)
10. For he is not a Jew, which is one _____ (2:28)
11. thou thyself art a guide of the _____, a light of them which are in darkness (2:19)
12. To them who by _____ continuance in well doing (2:7)
13. God shall judge the _____ of men (2:16)
15. Who will render to every man _____ to his deeds (2:6)
18. But glory, honour, and _____ (2:10)
21. But he is a Jew, which is one _____ (2:29)
22. whose _____ is not of men, but of God (2:29)
23. as many as have sinned in the law shall be _____ by the law (2:12)

Down

1. not knowing that the goodness of God leadeth thee to _____ (2:4)
2. being _____ out of the law (2:18)
3. the work of the law written in their hearts, their _____ also bearing witness (2:15)
7. circumcision is that of the _____, in the spirit (2:29)
9. For the name of God is _____ among the Gentiles (2:24)
14. do by nature the things _____ in the law (2:14)
15. Thou that sayest a man should not commit _____ (2:22)
16. For there is no _____ of persons with God (2:11)
17. the _____ of God is according to truth (2:2)
19. that thou shalt _____ the judgment of God (2:3)
20. But after thy _____ and impenitent heart (2:5)

All clues are taken directly from the 1611 edition of the King James Version (KJV).
Crossword Bible Studies - Romans (KJV) © 2012 Christy Bower
These puzzles are reproducible if you purchased the book.
www.CrosswordBibleStudies.com

Romans 2 (KJV)

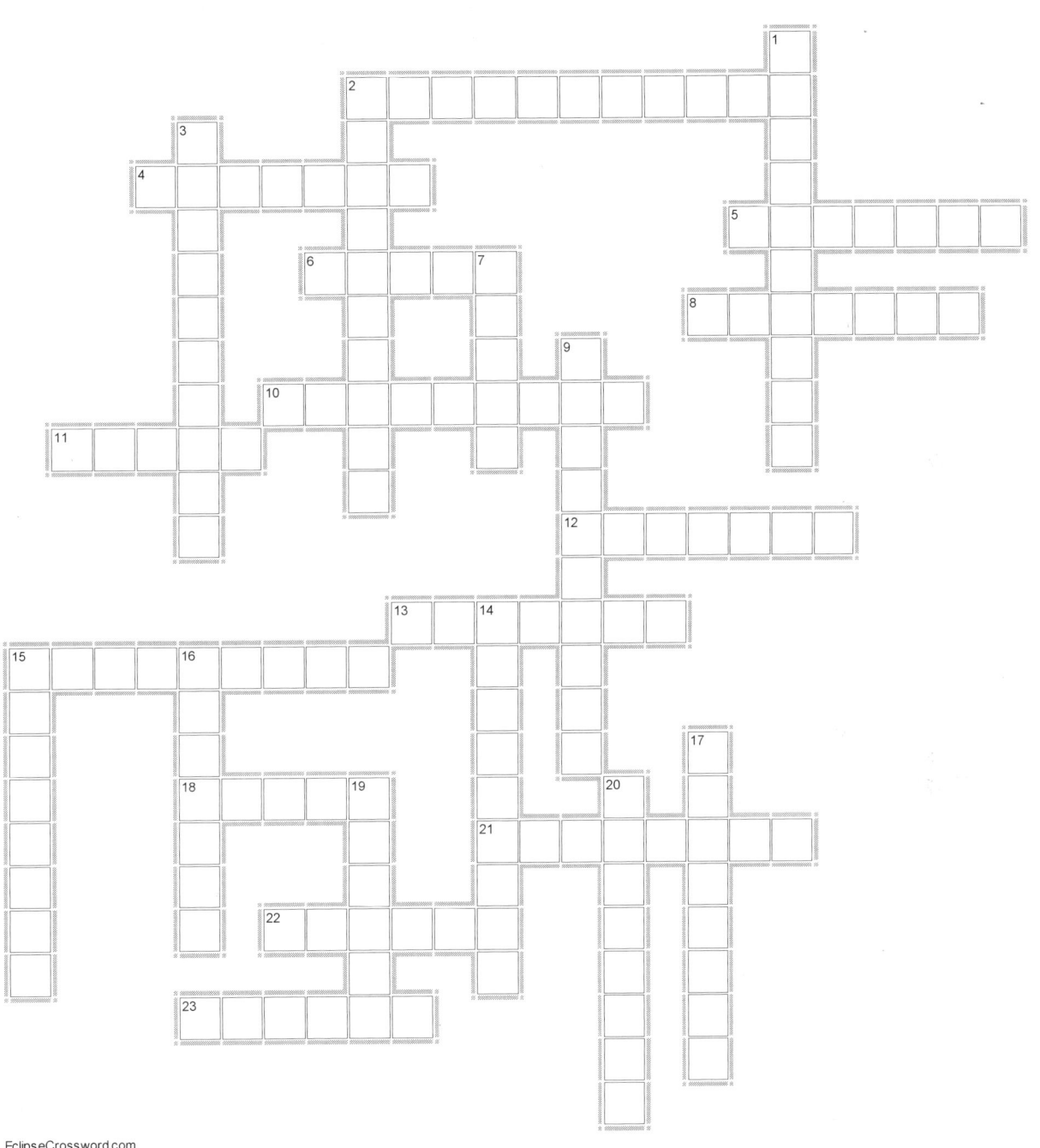

Romans 3 (KJV)

Across

3. _____ and misery are in their ways (3:16)
4. all the world may become _____ before God (3:19)
8. Is God unrighteous who taketh _____ (3:5)
9. There is no _____ of God before their eyes (3:18)
11. For if the _____ of God hath more abounded through my lie unto his glory (3:7)
16. through the _____ that is in Christ Jesus (3:24)
18. Let us do _____, that good may come (3:8)
19. for by the law is the _____ of sin (3:20)
21. shall their unbelief make the _____ of God without effect (3:3)
22. by the deeds of the law there shall no flesh be _____ in his sight (3:20)
24. But now the righteousness of God without the law is _____ (3:21)
25. Therefore we _____ that a man is justified by faith (3:28)
26. through the _____ of God (3:25)
27. There is none _____, no, not one (3:10)

Down

1. with their _____ they have used deceit; the poison of asps is under their lips (3:13)
2. Whose mouth is full of cursing and _____ (3:14)
5. they are together become _____; there is not that doeth good (3:12)
6. And the way of _____ have they not known (3:17)
7. To declare, I say, at this time his _____ (3:26)
10. Where is _____ then (3:27)
12. to declare his righteousness for the _____ of sins that are past (3:25)
13. For all have _____, and come short of the glory of God (3:23)
14. for then how shall God _____ the world (3:6)
15. Their feet are swift to shed _____ (3:15)
17. to be a _____ through faith in his blood (3:25)
20. for there is no _____ (3:22)
23. they are all under _____ (3:9)

All clues are taken directly from the 1611 edition of the King James Version (KJV).
Crossword Bible Studies - Romans (KJV) © 2012 Christy Bower
These puzzles are reproducible if you purchased the book.
www.CrosswordBibleStudies.com

Romans 3 (KJV)

Romans 4 (KJV)

Across

2. who also walk in the _____ of that faith of our father Abraham (4:12)
5. For the _____, that he should be the heir of the world (4:13)
6. I have made thee a _____ of many nations (4:17)
9. He _____ not at the promise of God through unbelief (4:20)
11. if we _____ on him that raised up Jesus our Lord from the dead (4:24)
12. Even as _____ also describeth the blessedness of the man (4:6)
16. Who was delivered for our offences, and was raised again for our _____ (4:25)
17. Therefore it is of faith, that it might be by _____ (4:16)
18. the father of all them that believe, though they be not _____ (4:11)
21. _____ is made void, and the promise is made of none effect (4:14)
22. when he was about an _____ years old (4:19)
24. And being not weak in faith, he _____ not his own body now dead (4:19)
25. for where no law is, there is no _____ (4:15)
26. that he might become the father of many _____ (4:18)

Down

1. Abraham _____ God, and it was counted unto him for righteousness (4:3)
3. _____ is the man to whom the Lord will not impute sin (4:8)
4. his faith is counted for _____ (4:5)
7. For if Abraham were _____ by works (4:2)
8. Now to him that worketh is the _____ not reckoned of grace (4:4)
10. faith was reckoned to _____ for righteousness (4:9)
13. And therefore it was _____ to him for righteousness (4:22)
14. Now it was not _____ for his sake alone (4:23)
15. And he _____ the sign of circumcision (4:11)
19. Blessed are they whose _____ are forgiven (4:7)
20. And being fully _____ that, what he had promised, he was able also to perform (4:21)
23. but was _____ in faith, giving glory to God (4:20)

All clues are taken directly from the 1611 edition of the King James Version (KJV).
Crossword Bible Studies - Romans (KJV) © 2012 Christy Bower
These puzzles are reproducible if you purchased the book.
www.CrosswordBibleStudies.com

Romans 4 (KJV)

Romans 5 (KJV)

Across

1. by the _____ of one the free gift came upon all men unto justification of life (5:18)
3. And _____, experience (5:4)
7. much more, being _____, we shall be saved by his life (5:10)
8. For as by one man's _____ many were made sinners (5:19)
9. being now justified by his _____ (5:9)
11. as by one man sin _____ into the world (5:12)
13. By whom also we have access by faith into this _____ wherein we stand (5:2)
15. by whom we have now received the _____ (5:11)
17. much more they which receive _____ of grace (5:17)
19. For scarcely for a _____ man will one die (5:7)
20. while we were yet _____, Christ died for us (5:8)
23. Therefore being _____ by faith, we have peace with God (5:1)
24. judgment came upon all men to _____ (5:18)
25. sin is not _____ when there is no law (5:13)

Down

2. and _____, hope (5:4)
4. But where sin _____, grace did much more abound (5:20)
5. knowing that _____ worketh patience (5:3)
6. _____ in hope of the glory of God (5:2)
10. so by the _____ of one shall many be made righteous (5:19)
12. over them that had not sinned after the similitude of Adam's _____ (5:14)
14. For if, when we were _____, we were reconciled to God by the death of his Son (5:10)
16. even so might grace reign through righteousness unto _____ life (5:21)
18. for the _____ was by one to condemnation (5:16)
21. That as sin hath _____ unto death (5:21)
22. the love of God is shed abroad in our _____ by the Holy Ghost (5:5)

All clues are taken directly from the 1611 edition of the King James Version (KJV).
Crossword Bible Studies - Romans (KJV) © 2012 Christy Bower
These puzzles are reproducible if you purchased the book.
www.CrosswordBibleStudies.com

Romans 5 (KJV)

Romans 6 (KJV)

Across

2. death hath no more _____ over him (6:9)
4. Now if we be dead with Christ, we _____ that we shall also live with him (6:8)
5. For the wages of sin is _____ (6:23)
6. Shall we _____ in sin, that grace may abound (6:1)
10. Know ye not, that so many of us as were _____ into Jesus Christ (6:3)
11. shall we sin, because we are not under the law, but under _____ (6:15)
13. but the gift of God is _____ life through Jesus Christ our Lord (6:23)
14. we also should walk in _____ of life (6:4)
16. dead indeed unto sin, but _____ unto God (6:11)
17. Let not sin therefore _____ in your mortal body (6:12)
18. ye have your fruit unto holiness, and the end _____ life (6:22)
20. What fruit had ye then in those things whereof ye are now _____ (6:21)
22. our old man is _____ with him (6:6)
23. that the body of sin might be _____ (6:6)
24. and your members as _____ of righteousness unto God (6:13)

Down

1. Neither yield ye your members as instruments of _____ unto sin (6:13)
3. as Christ was _____ up from the dead (6:4)
7. his servants ye are to whom ye _____ (6:16)
8. Being then made free from sin, ye became the servants of _____ (6:18)
9. ye were the servants of sin, but ye have _____ from the heart (6:17)
12. For when ye were the _____ of sin, ye were free from righteousness (6:20)
15. yield your members servants to righteousness unto _____ (6:19)
17. we shall be also in the likeness of his _____ (6:5)
19. But God be _____ (6:17)
21. For he that is _____ is freed from sin (6:7)

All clues are taken directly from the 1611 edition of the King James Version (KJV).
Crossword Bible Studies - Romans (KJV) © 2012 Christy Bower
These puzzles are reproducible if you purchased the book.
www.CrosswordBibleStudies.com

Romans 6 (KJV)

Romans 7 (KJV)

Across

1. I find then a law, that, when I would do good, evil is _____ with me (7:21)
2. ye should be _____ to another, even to him who is raised from the dead (7:4)
5. For the good that I would I do not: but the _____ which I would not, that I do (7:19)
6. For sin, taking _____ by the commandment, deceived me (7:11)
8. But sin, taking occasion by the _____ (7:8)
11. but when the commandment came, sin _____ (7:9)
12. So then with the mind I myself _____ the law of God; but with the flesh the law of sin (7:25)
13. God _____ (7:13)
14. the law is holy, and the commandment holy, and _____, and good (7:12)
17. For the woman which hath an _____ is bound by the law to her husband (7:2)
19. the law hath _____ over a man as long as he liveth (7:1)
22. But now we are _____ from the law (7:6)
23. If then I do that which I would not, I _____ unto the law that it is good (7:16)

Down

1. how to _____ that which is good I find not (7:18)
3. that we should serve in _____ of spirit, and not in the oldness of the letter (7:6)
4. Now then it is no more I that do it, but _____ that dwelleth in me (7:17)
7. bringing me into _____ to the law of sin which is in my members (7:23)
9. So then if, while her husband liveth, she be married to another man, she shall be called an _____ (7:3)
10. For I _____ in the law of God after the inward man (7:22)
13. For when we were in the _____ (7:5)
15. I am _____, sold under sin (7:14)
16. I _____ God through Jesus Christ our Lord (7:25)
18. who shall _____ me from the body of this death (7:24)
20. But I see another law in my _____, warring against the law of my mind (7:23)
21. for I had not known lust, except the law had said, Thou shalt not _____ (7:7)

All clues are taken directly from the 1611 edition of the King James Version (KJV).
Crossword Bible Studies - Romans (KJV) © 2012 Christy Bower
These puzzles are reproducible if you purchased the book.
www.CrosswordBibleStudies.com

Romans 7 (KJV)

Romans 8 (KJV)

Across

1. nor angels, nor _____, nor powers (8:38)
4. even we ourselves groan within ourselves, _____ for the adoption (8:23)
5. in all these things we are more than _____ through him that loved us (8:37)
6. For ye have not received the spirit of _____ again to fear (8:15)
7. For to be carnally minded is death; but to be _____ minded is life and peace (8:6)
9. And we know that all things work _____ for good to them that love God (8:28)
15. Because the _____ mind is enmity against God (8:7)
18. He that spared not his own Son, but _____ him up for us all (8:32)
19. but the Spirit itself maketh _____ for us with groanings which cannot be uttered (8:26)
21. For I reckon that the _____ of this present time (8:18)
23. Nor height, nor depth, nor any other _____, shall be able to separate us from the love of God (8:39)
24. Who shall _____ us from the love of Christ (8:35)
25. delivered from the bondage of corruption into the glorious _____ of the children of God (8:21)

Down

2. There is therefore now no _____ to them which are in Christ Jesus (8:1)
3. For as many as are led by the _____ of God, they are the sons of God (8:14)
8. For I am _____, that neither death nor life (8:38)
10. So then they that are in the flesh cannot _____ God (8:8)
11. but ye have received the Spirit of _____, whereby we cry, Abba, Father (8:15)
12. The Spirit itself beareth _____ with our spirit, that we are the children of God (8:16)
13. But if we hope for that we see not, then do we with _____ wait for it (8:25)
14. That the _____ of the law might be fulfilled in us (8:4)
16. If God be for us, who can be _____ us (8:31)
17. And he that searcheth the _____ knoweth what is the mind of the Spirit (8:27)
20. whom he called, them he also _____ (8:30)
22. Jesus hath made me _____ from the law of sin and death (8:2)

All clues are taken directly from the 1611 edition of the King James Version (KJV).
Crossword Bible Studies - Romans (KJV) © 2012 Christy Bower
These puzzles are reproducible if you purchased the book.
www.CrosswordBibleStudies.com

Romans 8 (KJV)

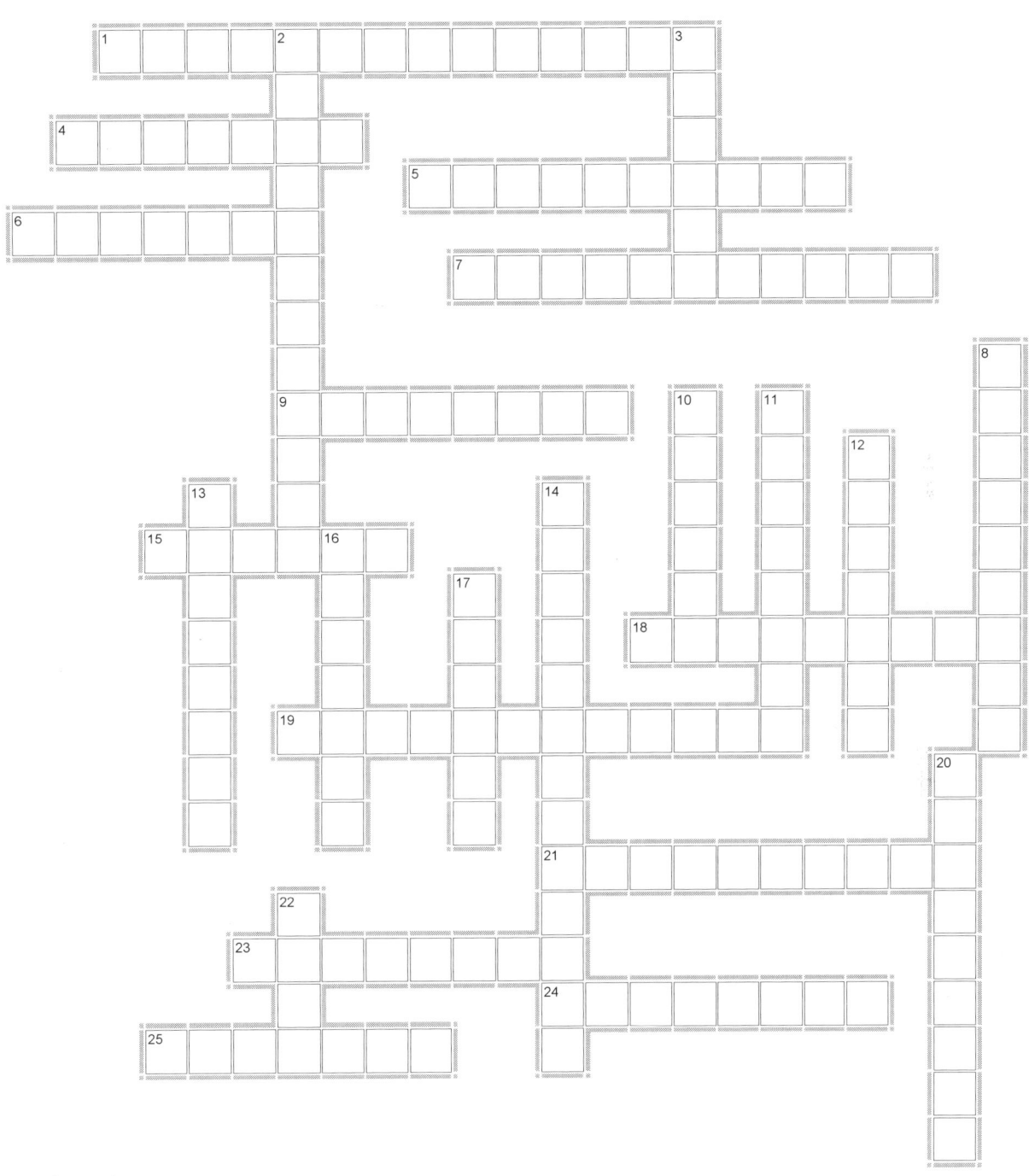

Romans 9 (KJV)

Across

4. But Israel, which followed after the law of _____, hath not attained to the law of righteousness (9:31)
6. For they _____ at the stumblingstone (9:32)
7. Not as though the _____ of God hath taken none effect (9:6)
10. Hath not the _____ power over the clay (9:21)
13. Jacob have I _____, but Esau have I hated (9:13)
14. What if God, willing to shew his wrath, and to make his _____ known (9:22)
15. there shall they be called the children of the _____ God (9:26)
16. Is there _____ with God? God forbid (9:14)
20. I will have mercy on whom I will have _____ (9:15)
23. They which are the _____ of the flesh, these are not the children of God (9:8)
24. Neither, because they are the seed of _____ (9:7)
25. For I could wish that myself were _____ from Christ for my brethren (9:3)

Down

1. For who hath _____ his will (9:19)
2. have attained to righteousness, even the righteousness which is of _____ (9:30)
3. my _____ also bearing me witness in the Holy Ghost (9:1)
5. Who are Israelites; to whom pertaineth the _____, and the glory, and the covenants (9:4)
8. Shall the thing _____ say to him that formed it, Why hast thou made me thus (9:20)
9. That I have great _____ and continual sorrow in my heart (9:2)
11. For this is the word of _____ (9:9)
12. and I will have compassion on whom I will have _____ (9:15)
17. And that he might make known the _____ of his glory (9:23)
18. For the _____ saith unto Pharaoh (9:17)
19. I will call them my _____, which were not my people (9:25)
21. The elder shall serve the _____ (9:12)
22. whosoever believeth on him shall not be _____ (9:33)

All clues are taken directly from the 1611 edition of the King James Version (KJV).
Crossword Bible Studies - Romans (KJV) © 2012 Christy Bower
These puzzles are reproducible if you purchased the book.
www.CrosswordBibleStudies.com

Romans 9 (KJV)

Romans 10 (KJV)

Across

3. For they being ignorant of God's _____ (10:3)
9. going about to establish their own righteousness, have not _____ themselves unto the righteousness of God (10:3)
10. my heart's desire and _____ to God for Israel is, that they might be saved (10:1)
12. and with the _____ confession is made unto salvation (10:10)
14. Who shall _____ into the deep (10:7)
16. For with the _____ man believeth unto righteousness (10:10)
18. I was made _____ unto them that asked not after me (10:20)
19. but not according to _____ (10:2)
22. and shalt _____ in thine heart that God hath raised him from the dead (10:9)
23. Whosoever believeth on him shall not be _____ (10:11)
24. I will provoke you to _____ (10:19)
25. But the righteousness which is of _____ (10:6)

Down

1. For there is no _____ between the Jew and the Greek (10:12)
2. they have a _____ of God (10:2)
4. thou shalt be _____ (10:9)
5. How beautiful are the feet of them that preach the _____ of peace (10:15)
6. that is, the word of faith, which we _____ (10:8)
7. Who shall _____ into heaven (10:6)
8. their sound went into all the earth, and their words unto the ends of the _____ (10:18)
11. All day long I have stretched forth my hands unto a _____ and gainsaying people (10:21)
13. But they have not all _____ the gospel (10:16)
15. For whosoever shall call upon the _____ of the Lord shall be saved (10:13)
17. That if thou shalt _____ with thy mouth (10:9)
20. how shall they hear without a _____ (10:14)
21. So then faith cometh by _____ (10:17)

All clues are taken directly from the 1611 edition of the King James Version (KJV).
Crossword Bible Studies - Romans (KJV) © 2012 Christy Bower
These puzzles are reproducible if you purchased the book.
www.CrosswordBibleStudies.com

Romans 10 (KJV)

Romans 11 (KJV)

Across

1. Now if the fall of them be the riches of the _____ (11:12)
4. Let their table be made a snare, and a trap, and a _____ (11:9)
6. Boast not against the _____ (11:18)
7. For this is my _____ unto them, when I shall take away their sins (11:27)
8. But if it be of _____, then is it no more grace (11:6)
9. For as ye in times past have not believed God, yet have now _____ mercy through their unbelief (11:30)
10. Behold therefore the _____ and severity of God (11:22)
11. For the gifts and _____ of God are without repentance (11:29)
15. For who hath known the mind of the Lord? or who hath been his _____ (11:34)
17. There shall come out of Sion the _____ (11:26)
18. _____ in part is happened to Israel (11:25)
22. through their fall _____ is come unto the Gentiles (11:11)
24. because of _____ they were broken off (11:20)
25. and shall turn away _____ from Jacob (11:26)
26. Or who hath first given to him, and it shall be _____ unto him again (11:35)
27. Let their eyes be _____, that they may not see (11:10)

Down

2. For if the casting away of them be the _____ of the world (11:15)
3. how he maketh _____ to God against Israel (11:2)
5. O the depth of the riches both of the wisdom and _____ of God (11:33)
12. I am the _____ of the Gentiles (11:13)
13. The branches were _____ off (11:19)
14. how _____ are his judgments, and his ways past finding out (11:33)
16. As concerning the _____, they are enemies for your sakes (11:28)
19. there is a remnant according to the _____ of grace (11:5)
20. For if thou wert cut out of the _____ tree which is wild by nature (11:24)
21. with them partakest of the root and _____ of the olive tree (11:17)
23. If by any means I may _____ to emulation them which are my flesh (11:14)

Romans 11 (KJV)

Romans 12 (KJV)

Across

1. _____ is mine; I will repay, saith the Lord (12:19)
3. he that sheweth mercy, with _____ (12:8)
4. For as we have many _____ in one body (12:4)
6. _____ to the necessity of the saints (12:13)
11. holy, acceptable unto God, which is your _____ service (12:1)
12. weep with them that _____ (12:15)
15. for in so doing thou shalt heap coals of fire on his _____ (12:20)
16. Having then gifts _____ according to the grace that is given to us (12:6)
19. he that giveth, let him do it with _____ (12:8)
20. And be not _____ to this world (12:2)
21. Dearly beloved, _____ not yourselves, but rather give place unto wrath (12:19)
23. Be not overcome of evil, but _____ evil with good (12:21)

Down

2. For I say, through the _____ given unto me (12:3)
3. So we, being many, are one body in _____ (12:5)
5. Bless them which _____ you (12:14)
7. _____ to no man evil for evil (12:17)
8. but be ye _____ by the renewing of your mind (12:2)
9. present your bodies a living _____ (12:1)
10. _____ in hope; patient in tribulation (12:12)
13. not to think of himself more _____ than the ought to think (12:3)
14. Be not _____ in your own conceits (12:16)
17. If it be possible, as much as lieth in you, live _____ with all men (12:18)
18. Be kindly affectioned one to another with _____ love (12:10)
21. Be of the same mind one toward _____ (12:16)
22. if thine enemy _____, feed him (12:20)

All clues are taken directly from the 1611 edition of the King James Version (KJV).
Crossword Bible Studies - Romans (KJV) © 2012 Christy Bower
These puzzles are reproducible if you purchased the book.
www.CrosswordBibleStudies.com

Romans 12 (KJV)

All clues are taken directly from the 1611 edition of the King James Version (KJV).
Crossword Bible Studies - Romans (KJV) © 2012 Christy Bower
These puzzles are reproducible if you purchased the book.
www.CrosswordBibleStudies.com

Romans 13 (KJV)

Across

3. Whosoever therefore resisteth the power, resisteth the _____ of God (13:2)
7. For he is a _____ of God to thee for good (13:4)
9. _____ therefore to all their dues (13:7)
14. therefore love is the _____ of the law (13:10)
15. for now is our _____ nearer than when we believed (13:11)
16. let us therefore cast off the works of _____ (13:12)
20. and if there be any other _____ (13:9)
23. But put ye on the Lord Jesus Christ, and make not _____ for the flesh (13:14)
24. and let us put on the armour of _____ (13:12)
25. not in chambering and wantonness, not in strive and _____ (13:13)

Down

1. Thou shalt not _____ adultery (13:9)
2. _____ worketh no ill to his neighbour (13:10)
4. it is briefly _____ in this saying (13:9)
5. tribute to whom tribute is due; _____ to whom custom (13:7)
6. for he that loveth another hath _____ the law (13:8)
8. But if thou do that which is evil, be _____ (13:4)
10. ye must needs be subject, not only for wrath, but also for _____ sake (13:5)
11. For there is no _____ but of God (13:1)
12. he is the minister of God, a _____ to execute wrath upon him that doeth evil (13:4)
13. For _____ are not a terror to good works (13:3)
17. Let every soul be _____ unto the higher powers (13:1)
18. they that resist shall receive to themselves _____ (13:2)
19. Let us walk _____, as in the day (13:13)
21. Owe no man any thing, but to love one _____ (13:8)
22. for this cause pay ye _____ also (13:6)

All clues are taken directly from the 1611 edition of the King James Version (KJV).
Crossword Bible Studies - Romans (KJV) © 2012 Christy Bower
These puzzles are reproducible if you purchased the book.
www.CrosswordBibleStudies.com

Romans 13 (KJV)

Romans 14 (KJV)

Across

2. and things wherewith one may _____ another (14:19)
5. Let us therefore follow after the things which make for _____ (14:19)
7. He that eateth, eateth to the Lord, for he giveth God _____ (14:6)
10. but _____, and peace, and joy in the Holy Ghost (14:17)
11. for whatsoever is not of faith is _____ (14:23)
12. For the _____ of God is not meat and drink (14:17)
13. for we shall all stand before the _____ seat of Christ (14:10)
15. every one of us shall give _____ of himself to God (14:12)
16. whereby thy brother stumbleth, or is _____, or is made weak (14:21)
18. For none of us liveth to _____, and no one dieth to himself (14:7)
20. For one believeth that he may eat all _____ (14:1)
21. whether we live _____, or die, we are the Lord's (14:8)
22. _____ not the work of God (14:20)

Down

1. every _____ shall bow to me (14:11)
3. And he that doubteth is _____ if he eat, because he eateth not of faith (14:23)
4. that no man put a _____ or an occasion to fall in his brother's way (14:13)
6. acceptable to God, and _____ of men (14:18)
7. and every _____ shall confess to God (14:11)
8. Let every man be fully _____ in his own mind (14:5)
9. Lord both of the dead and _____ (14:9)
11. Yea, he shall be holden up: for God is able to make him _____ (14:4)
14. But if thy brother is _____ with thy meat (14:15)
15. For he that in these things serveth Christ is _____ to God (14:18)
17. Let not him that eateth _____ him that eateth not (14:3)
19. Him that is weak in the _____ receive ye (14:1)

All clues are taken directly from the 1611 edition of the King James Version (KJV).
Crossword Bible Studies - Romans (KJV) © 2012 Christy Bower
These puzzles are reproducible if you purchased the book.
www.CrosswordBibleStudies.com

Romans 14 (KJV)

Romans 15 (KJV)

Across

2. having a great _____ these many years to come unto you (15:23)
5. to make a certain _____ for the poor saints which are at Jerusalem (15:26)
7. I shall come in the fulness of the _____ of the gospel of Christ (15:29)
10. Through mighty signs and _____ (15:19)
11. Now I say that Jesus Christ was a _____ (15:8)
12. For which cause also I have been much _____ from coming to you (15:22)
14. that my service which I have for Jerusalem may be _____ of the saints (15:31)
15. Whensoever I take my _____ into Spain (15:24)
17. _____ the Lord, all ye Gentiles; and laud him, all ye people (15:11)
20. But now I go unto _____ to minister unto the saints (15:25)
22. that the offering up of the Gentiles might be acceptable, being _____ by the Holy Ghost (15:16)
24. because of the _____ that is given to me of God (15:15)
25. through the _____ of the Holy Ghost (15:13)
26. that ye also are full of goodness, filled with all knowledge, able also to _____ one another (15:14)
27. Let every one of us please his neighbour for his good to _____ (15:2)

Down

1. Now the God of hope fill you with all joy and _____ in believing (15:13)
3. That I may come unto you with joy by the will of God, and may with you be _____ (15:32)
4. lest I should build upon another man's _____ (15:20)
6. We then that are strong ought to bear the _____ of the weak (15:1)
8. that ye may _____ in hope (15:13)
9. Now the God of _____ and consolation grant you to be likeminded (15:5)
13. that ye strive together with me in your _____ to God for me (15:30)
16. _____, ye Gentiles, with his people (15:10)
18. For if the Gentiles have been made _____ of their spiritual things (15:27)
19. And I myself also am _____ of you (15:14)
21. For whatsoever things were written aforetime were written for our _____ (15:4)
23. I have fully _____ the gospel of Christ (15:19)

Romans 15 (KJV)

Romans 16 (KJV)

Across

1. made known to all _____ for the obedience of faith (16:26)
4. For your _____ is come abroad unto all men (16:19)
6. For they that are such _____ not our Lord Jesus Christ (16:18)
9. Erastus the _____ of the city saluteth you (16:23)
10. I commend unto you _____ our sister (16:1)
13. assist her in whatsoever _____ she hath need of you (16:2)
15. Written to the _____ from Corinthus, and sent by Phebe (16:27)
18. according to the commandment of the _____ God (16:26)
20. according to the revelation of the _____, which was kept secret since the world began (16:25)
22. Greet Priscilla and _____ my helpers in Christ Jesus (16:3)
23. Salute Apelles _____ in Christ (16:10)
24. Salute Herodion my _____ (16:11)
25. I Tertius, who wrote this _____, salute you in the Lord (16:22)

Down

2. But now is made manifest, and by the _____ of the prophets (16:26)
3. by good words and fair speeches _____ the hearts of the simple (16:18)
5. Likewise greet the _____ that is in their house (16:5)
7. _____ the beloved Persis, which laboured much in the Lord (16:12)
8. Greet Amplias my _____ in the Lord (16:8)
11. And the God of peace shall _____ Satan under your feet shortly (16:20)
12. Salute one _____ with an holy kiss (16:16)
14. To God only wise, be _____ through Jesus Christ for ever (16:27)
16. Salute Urbane, our _____ in Christ (16:9)
17. mark them which cause _____ and offences (16:17)
19. The _____ of our Lord Jesus Christ (16:24)
21. and all the _____ which are with them (16:15)

All clues are taken directly from the 1611 edition of the King James Version (KJV).
Crossword Bible Studies - Romans (KJV) © 2012 Christy Bower
These puzzles are reproducible if you purchased the book.
www.CrosswordBibleStudies.com

Romans 16 (KJV)

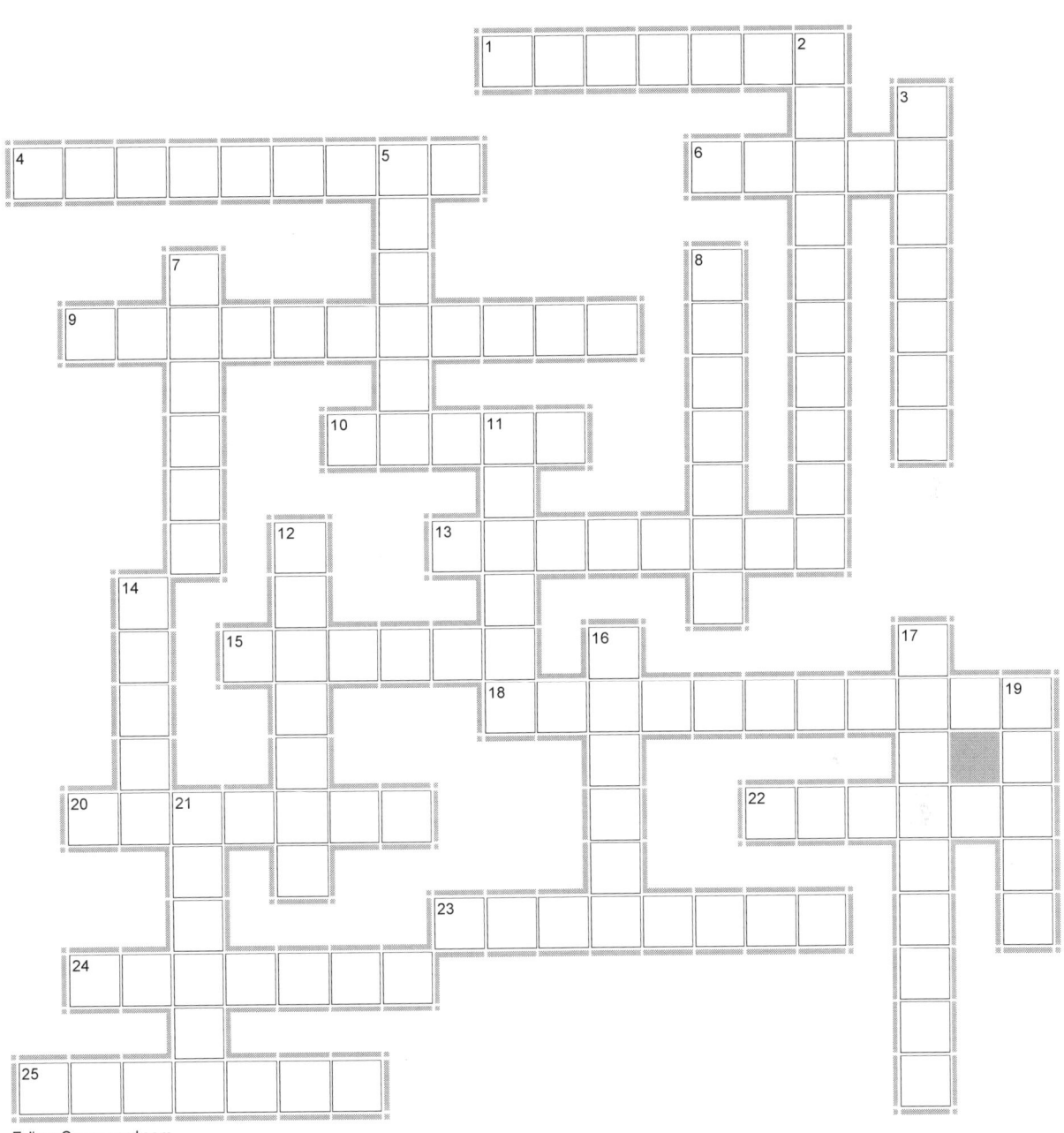

EclipseCrossword.com

All clues are taken directly from the 1611 edition of the King James Version (KJV).
Crossword Bible Studies - Romans (KJV) © 2012 Christy Bower
These puzzles are reproducible if you purchased the book.
www.CrosswordBibleStudies.com

Solutions

Romans 1 (KJV)

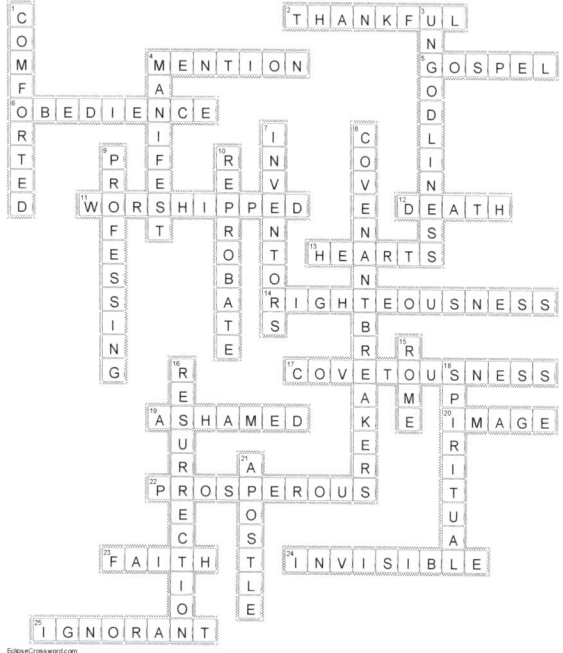

Romans 3 (KJV)

Romans 2 (KJV)

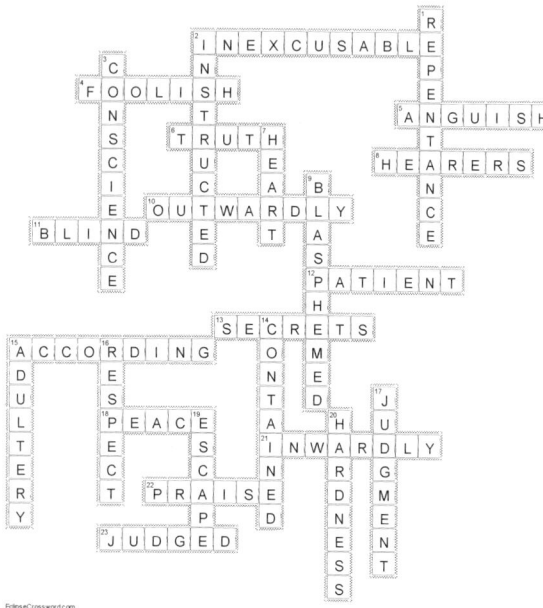

Romans 4 (KJV)

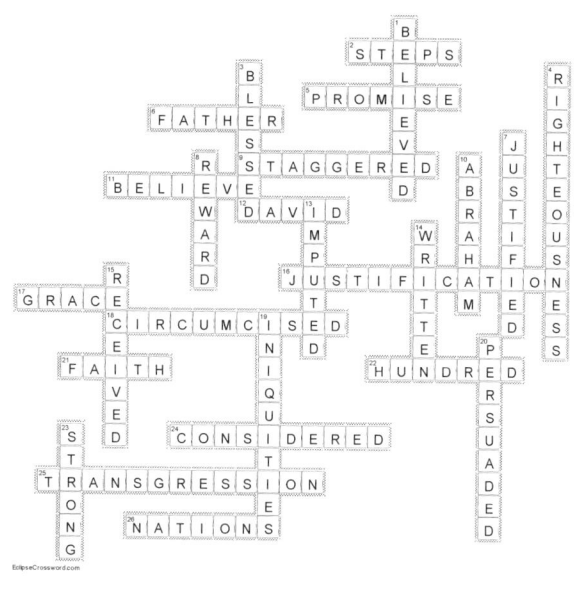

All clues are taken directly from the 1611 edition of the King James Version (KJV).
Crossword Bible Studies - Romans (KJV) © 2012 Christy Bower
These puzzles are reproducible if you purchased the book.
www.CrosswordBibleStudies.com

Romans 5 (KJV)

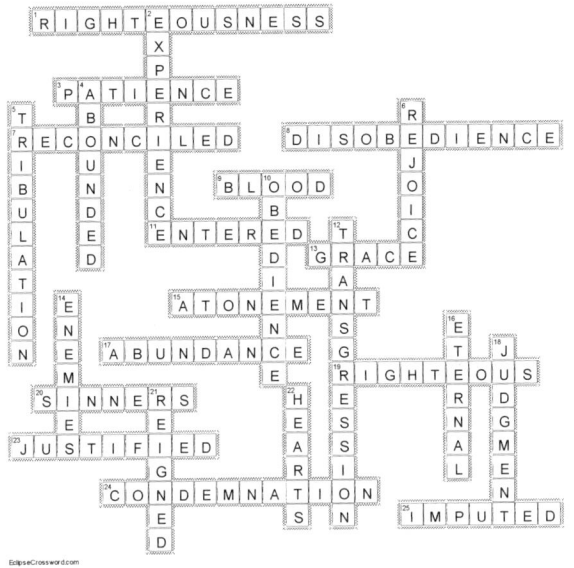

Romans 7 (KJV)

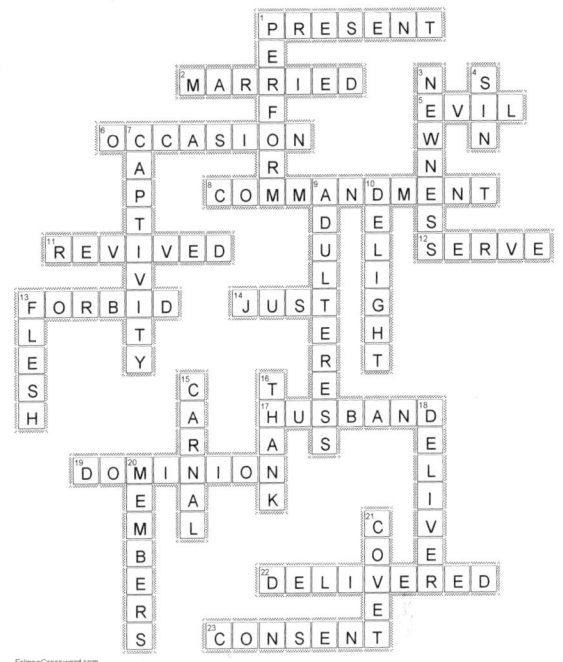

Romans 6 (KJV)

Romans 8 (KJV)

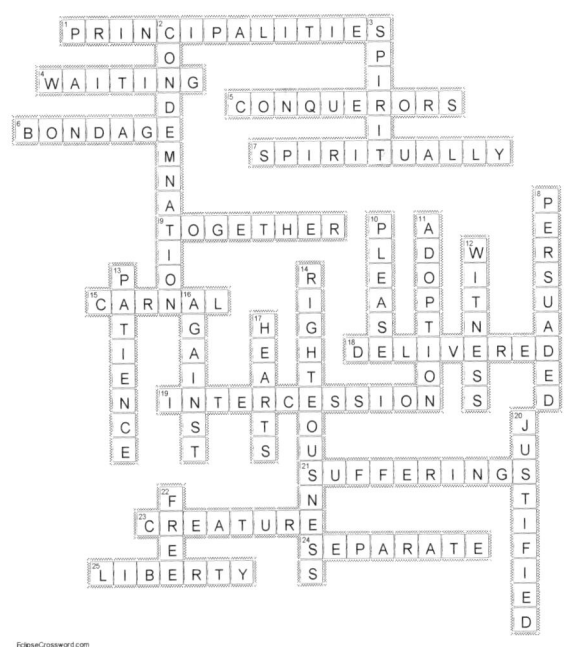

All clues are taken directly from the 1611 edition of the King James Version (KJV).
Crossword Bible Studies - Romans (KJV) © 2012 Christy Bower
These puzzles are reproducible if you purchased the book.

www.CrosswordBibleStudies.com

Romans 9 (KJV)

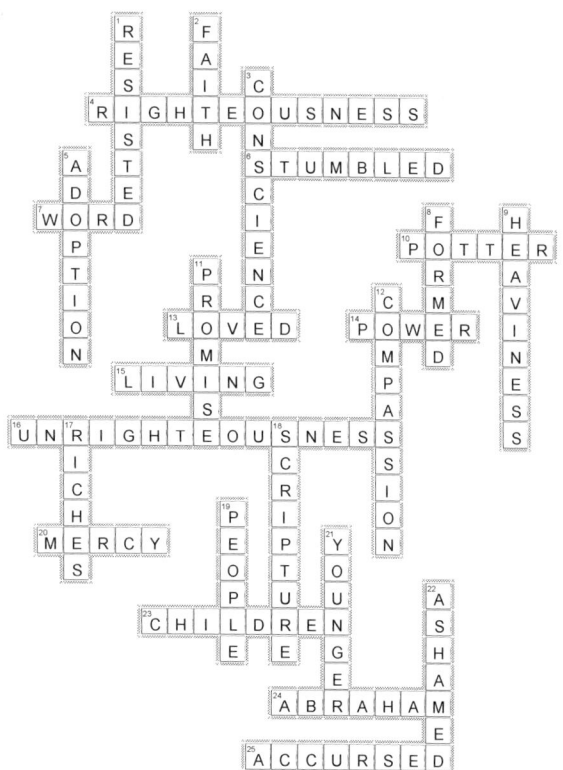

Romans 11 (KJV)

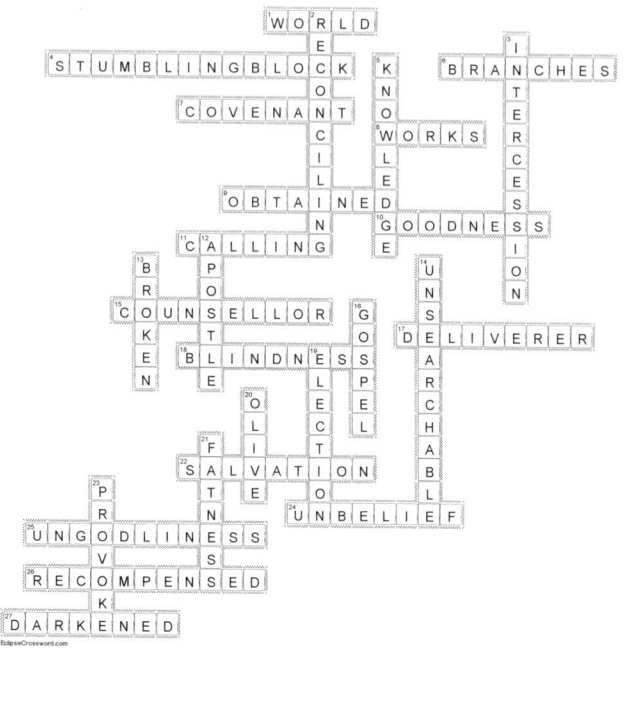

Romans 10 (KJV)

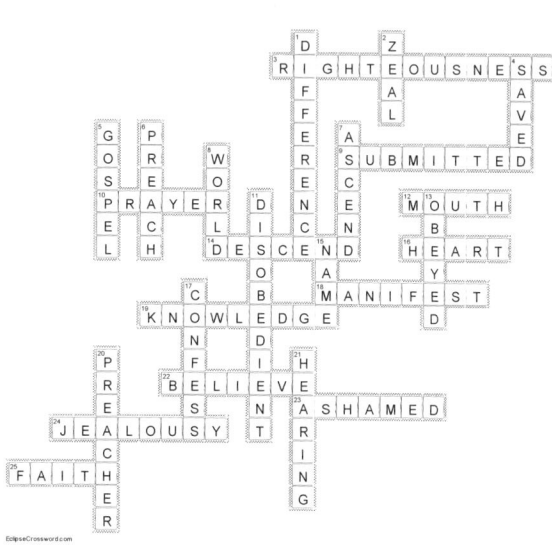

Romans 12 (KJV)

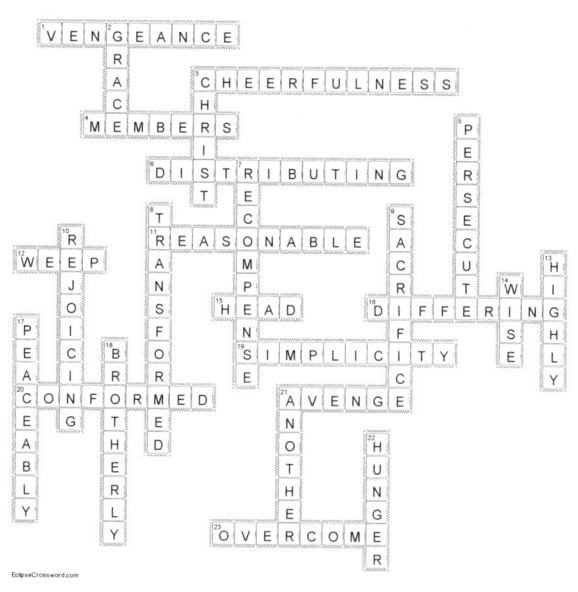

All clues are taken directly from the 1611 edition of the King James Version (KJV).
Crossword Bible Studies - Romans (KJV) © 2012 Christy Bower
These puzzles are reproducible if you purchased the book.
www.CrosswordBibleStudies.com

Romans 13 (KJV)

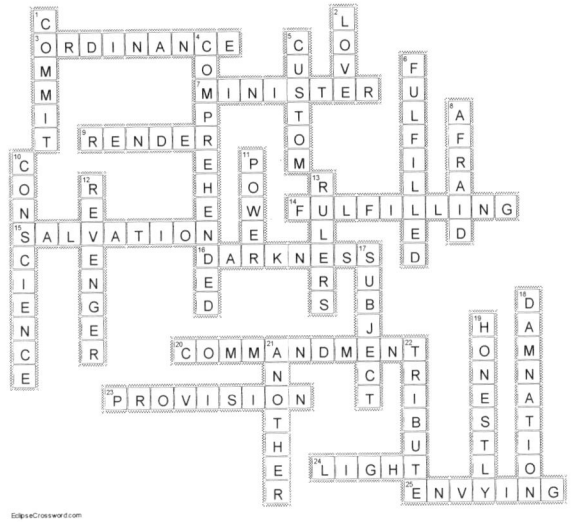

Romans 15 (KJV)

Romans 14 (KJV)

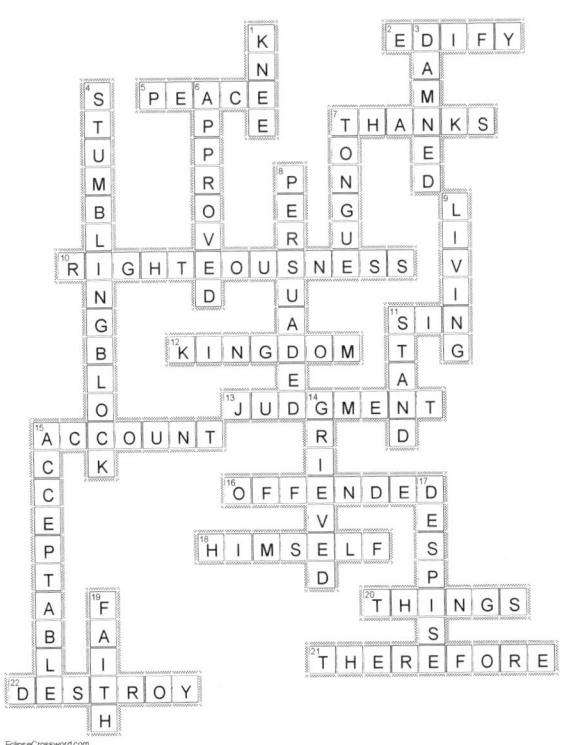

Romans 16 (KJV)

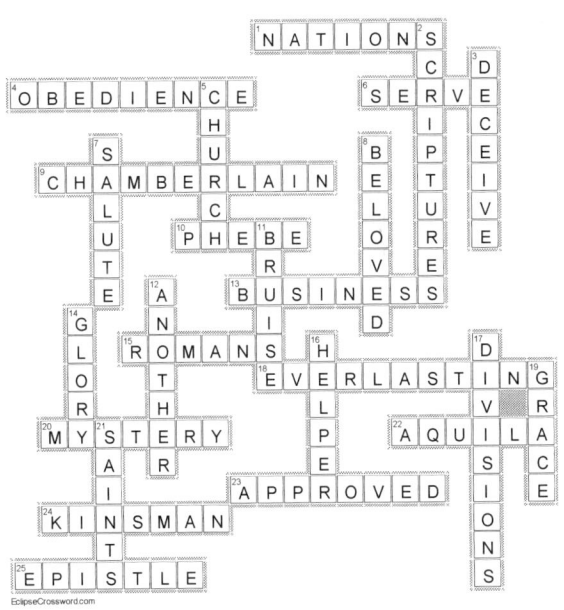

All clues are taken directly from the 1611 edition of the King James Version (KJV).
Crossword Bible Studies - Romans (KJV) © 2012 Christy Bower
These puzzles are reproducible if you purchased the book.
www.CrosswordBibleStudies.com

Made in the USA
Columbia, SC
19 September 2018